Medicine c

Prayers and Meditations for Mass and Eucharistic
Adoration

Fr. John J. Pasquini, Th.D.

Quotes from the Fathers of the Church are found in the following: Jurgens, William A. ed. and trans. *The Faith of the Early Fathers*. 3 vols. Collegeville: The Liturgical Press, 1970; *The Apostolic Fathers: The Loeb Classical Library*. 2 vols. Edited by G.P. Goold and translated by Kirsopp Lake. Cambridge: Harvard University Press, 1998. Bible quotes are from NABRE, unless otherwise cited.

Nihil Obstat
Rev. Dennis M. Duvelius
Censor Liborum
Archdiocese of Indianapolis

Imprimatur
Rev. Msgr. Joseph F. Schaedel
Vicar General/Moderator of the Curia
Archdiocese of Indianapolis
June 10, 2007

Veritas Publications and Press
Originally published by S of C Publications
All rights, Fr. John J. Pasquini

Printed in the United States of America

Table of Contents

Cardinal Endorsements   5

Introduction: Theology of Eucharist   7

Prayers and Meditations   23

Appendix: Benediction   127

To Florence, my mother, the love of my life.

Cardinal Endorsements

"Fr. John Pasquini's *Medicine of Immortality* is a wonderful source of inspiration for priests, and all who read it, to gain a deeper appreciation of the healing power of the Eucharist. His clear, succinct presentation of the Mass offers a pastorally insightful explanation of the mystery we believe, we celebrate and which we are called to live out in our lives. The prayers and meditations compiled in this book offer opportunities for spiritual reflection which will assist the reader in growth toward a deeper understanding of the mystery of the Eucharist."

Anthony Cardinal Bevilacqua
Archbishop Emeritus of Philadelphia

"In *Medicine of Immortality*, Father John Pasquini offers his readers the richness of Catholic devotional prayer, the wisdom of the Fathers and, most of all, the fruits of his own prayer and meditation before the Blessed Sacrament. I recommend this book to all who wish to grow in their love for the Lord, who sustains the life of His Church through the precious gift of His Body and Blood."

Francis Cardinal George, O.M.I.
Archbishop Emeritus of Chicago

Theology of the Eucharist

Eucharist as Resurrected Body and Blood of Jesus

If the words of Elijah had power to bring down fire from heaven, will not the words of Christ have power to change the natures of the elements [of bread and wine into the body and blood of Jesus]?

...The Lord Jesus himself declares: This is my body. Before the blessing contained in these words a different thing is named, [bread]; after the consecration a body is indicated. He himself speaks of his blood. Before the consecration something else is spoken of, [wine]; after the consecration blood is designated.

Ambrose (397d), On the Mysteries
(Cf. Nm. 52-54, 58: SC 25 bis, 186-188. 190)

Jesus came to us in Bethlehem, which means "house of bread," and was placed in a "manger" which is an eating vessel. Today Jesus is present in the tabernacle, those houses where the bread of eternal life, the body, blood, soul and divinity of Christ is present throughout the world. He is given to us in a manger, an eating vessel, the chalice and the paten at every Mass. From the very moment of his incarnation, his entrance into the world, the Son of God was pointing to his wonderful gift of the Eucharist!

Belief in the Eucharist as the Body and Blood of Christ has declined in recent years. This is the sad consequence of the growth of secularism, modernism, and fundamentalism.

Despite this, the Scriptures and Tradition affirm the Catholic position on the Eucharist. Let us examine a powerful passage from the Bible:

The Jews...disputed among themselves, saying, "How can this man give us his flesh to eat?" So Jesus said to them, "Truly, truly, I say to you, unless you eat the flesh of the Son of man and drink his blood, you have no life in you; he who eats my flesh and drinks my blood has eternal life, and I will raise him up at the last day. For my flesh is food indeed and my blood is drink indeed. He who eats my flesh and drinks my blood abides in me, and I in him. As the living Father sent me, and I live because of the Father, so he who eats me will live because of me. This is the bread that came down from heaven, not such as the fathers ate and died; he who eats this bread will live forever.... Many of his disciples, when they heard it, said, "This is a hard saying; who can listen to it?" ...After this many of his disciples drew back and no longer went about with him (Jn. 6:52-58; 60; 66, RSV; also make reference to the following passages: Mt. 26:26-28; Mk. 14:22-24; Lk. 22:19f; 1 Cor. 10:16; 11:24f; 27; 29).*

John's Gospel emphasizes not just the "body," but the "flesh" of Christ that one is called to partake in. Furthermore, when one looks at the word that John uses for "eat," the word that John uses is not the classical Greek word for eat, rather it is--during this particular time in history--a vulgar term used to describe animals eating. The best translation today would probably be "munch" or "gnaw." Obviously John is emphasizing the reality of the Body and Blood of Christ as something tangible.

Some like to emphasize the fact that Jesus called himself a door (Jn. 10:9), a vine (Jn. 15:1), a lamb (Jn. 1:29), a light (Jn. 8:12), living water (Jn. 4:14), etc. They would claim that Jesus was being symbolic here. They would argue consequently that Jesus in referring to the Eucharist as his Body and Blood was doing no different than calling himself living water.

While it is true there is a symbolic dimension to calling Jesus the Bread of Life, the early Christians, however, understood that Jesus was referring to that which transcended the simply symbolic. Jesus was talking about his Real Presence in the Eucharist, his real Body and Blood.

When we look to history, we recognize that Christians were often sent to their deaths by the Romans under the accusation of being cannibals—as testified to by the 1st century pagan historian Tacitus in his *Annals*. Where would they get such a thought unless the Real Presence was not obviously and fervently believed? (What Tacitus did not realize is that Catholics eat the Risen Christ! Cannibals eat dead flesh).

No one went to his or her death for proclaiming Jesus as a door, a vine, a lamb, or symbolic bread. No one went to his or her death in the amphitheater for worshiping a door or living water. The early Church always distinguished that which was symbolic from that which was to be taken literally. Acts 10:39 describes Jesus as being hung on a tree; all Christians knew he had been crucified on a cross; all Christians knew that Paul was using symbolic language.

It is also interesting to read that after Jesus' discourse on the Bread of Life, many of the disciples abandoned him. *Why would they abandon him if all they thought was that Jesus was using symbolic language?* Why run away if all that is being talked about is a symbol?

The disciples knew that Jesus was not simply talking symbolically. That is why they ran away! Genesis 9:3-4 and Leviticus 17:14 strongly forbade the eating or drinking of blood. The disciples abandoned Jesus because they knew of these quotes from the Old Testament and they knew that Jesus was talking literally.

The disciples never abandoned Jesus for being the "door," the "vine," the "lamb," or "the Son of God." They never abandoned Jesus when he said he was the way, the truth, and the life, and that no one goes to God the Father except through him (Jn. 14:6). Nor did they abandon him for forgiving sins or working on the Sabbath, which only God can do! But they certainly ran away when they heard

Jesus describe his Real Presence in the Eucharist.

Whenever in the Scriptures there was confusion among his disciples, Jesus corrected the misunderstanding and explained to them the true meaning of what he meant (see Jn. 3:3-5; Jn. 11:11-14; Mt. 19:24-26; Jn. 8:21-23; Jn. 8:31-36; Jn. 6:32-35). And when Jesus wanted his words to be taken literally he repeated and reaffirmed what he said (see Mt. 9:2-6; Jn. 8:56-59; Jn. 6:41-51).

Jesus, in this Eucharistic passage, not only does not explain away what he says, he re-enforces the literal meaning of what he is saying by repeating it over and over again. In fact, Jesus repeats six times in six verses the same literal truth (Jn. 6:53-58). Jesus wants to make the point perfectly clear. Notice, that Jesus does not run after the departing disciples and say, "Wait a minute, you misunderstood what I said! I was only talking symbolically!" Rather, he turned to the remaining disciples and said, "Are you going to leave me too" (Jn. 6:67)?

Now some like to point to verse 64 where we read, "It is the spirit that gives life, while the flesh is of no avail." They claim this proves that Jesus was only talking symbolically since flesh is "of no avail."

This argument makes no philosophical sense. Would Jesus at one moment be saying "eat my flesh" and then in the next moment be saying, "but my flesh is no good?" That would simply be illogical!

John 6:64 must be understood as John 3:6 is understood; that is, only by a gift of God can one truly comprehend and believe in what Jesus has said. Only by a gift from above, the gift of the Spirit, can one believe in the Real Presence of Christ in the Eucharist, for "no one can come to [Jesus] unless it is granted him by my Father" (Jn. 6:65).

Now one may argue, "How can Jesus be present in different ways?" That should be easy to answer for all Christians. Christ is present in the individual, in the congregation, in the minister, in the proclamation of the Word and so on. So too, Christ is sacramentally present in the

Eucharist.

Let us examine one more powerful passage:

[A]nyone who eats the bread and drinks the cup of the Lord unworthily is answerable for the body and blood of the Lord. Everyone is to examine himself and only then eat of the bread or drink from the cup, because a person who eats and drinks without recognizing the body is eating and drinking his own condemnation (1 Cor.11:27-29, NJB).

Can a symbol bring one's own condemnation? Paul gets right to the point. We are dealing with the Real Presence of Christ in the Eucharist under the appearance, or what is technically called the "species" of bread and wine.

Let us now look at one who walked and talked and learned from the apostles themselves. What did he believe about the Eucharist? Would you believe the word of a person who lived in the sixteenth century who had no personal contact with an apostle or would you prefer the word of one who was taught by an apostle? I suspect that we would all prefer the testimony of a person that learned his Christianity from one of the apostles.

Ignatius of Antioch (ca. 107), the disciple of John and friend of Peter and Paul, writing only seven years after the death of the apostle John, reprimands the Docetists in his letter to the *Smyrneans* (6:7) for failing to believe in Christ's Real Presence in the Eucharist:

For let nobody be under any delusion; there is judgment in store for the hosts of heaven, even the very angels in glory, the visible and invisible powers themselves, if they have no faith in the blood of Christ. Let him who can, absorb this truth.... But look at the men who have those perverted notions about the grace of Jesus Christ which has come down to us, and see how contrary to the mind of God they are. They even absent themselves from the

Eucharist and from prayer because they do not confess that the Eucharist is the flesh of our Savior Jesus Christ....

In another passage, Ignatius reminds us that there is only one authentic Eucharist:

Be careful...to use one Eucharist, for there is one flesh of our Lord Jesus Christ, and one cup for union with his blood, one altar, as there is one bishop with the presbytery [priesthood] and the deacons my fellow servants, in order that whatever you do you may do it according to God (*Philadelphia*, 4, trans. Lake).

In another passage to the Romans, Ignatius writes:

I have no taste for corruptible food nor for the pleasure of this life. I desire the Bread of God, which is the Flesh of Jesus Christ, who was of the seed of David; and for drink I desire His Blood, which is love incorruptible (*Romans, 7:3, Jurgens*).

Ignatius of Antioch is a giant in Christendom. His words were recognized as truth, for they came from the mouth of a disciple of the apostles John, Peter, and Paul.

Irenaeus, the friend of Polycarp, who in turn was the friend of the apostle John wrote:

Jesus declared the cup, a part of creation, to be His own Blood, from which He causes our blood to flow; and the bread, a part of creation, He has established as His own Body, from which He gives increase to our bodies (*Against Heresies 5, 2, 2*).

Justin Martyr, well-known by the disciples of the apostle John, wrote:

We call this food Eucharist...since Jesus Christ our Savior was made incarnate by the word of God and had both flesh and blood for our salvation, so too, as we have been taught, the food which has been made into the Eucharist by the Eucharistic prayer set down by Him, and by the change of which our blood and flesh is nourished, is both the flesh and the blood of that incarnated Jesus.

Justin further goes on to say:

None is allowed to share in the Eucharist unless he believes the things which we teach are true...for we do not receive the Eucharist as ordinary bread and ordinary wine, but as Jesus Christ our Savior.

Cyril of Jerusalem, another man acquainted with the disciples of John, wrote:

[Jesus] himself...having declared and said of the Bread, "This is My Body," who will dare any longer to doubt? And when He Himself has affirmed and said, "This is my Blood," who can ever hesitate and say it is not His Blood" (Catechetical Lectures 22, Mystagogic 4).

Do not, therefore, regard the bread and wine as simply that, for they are, according to the Master's declaration, the Body and Blood of Christ. Even though the senses suggest to you the other, let faith make you firm. Do not judge in this matter by taste, but be fully assured by faith, not doubting that you have been deemed worthy of the Body and Blood of Christ (Ibid.).

The Real Presence of Christ in the Eucharist has always been held. No one seriously or significantly questioned the

Real Presence of Christ until the eleventh century with the writings of Berengarius of Tours. Would God allow eleven centuries to go by with a false belief? Since Jesus said he would be with the Church for all eternity (Mt. 16:18; 28:20), then he would not allow it to enter into error.

How sad it must be for those who do not receive the real Eucharist for it is, as Ignatius says in *Ephesians* 20, "the medicine of immortality, the antidote that we shall not die, but live forever in Jesus Christ."

Before we move on to the nature of the Mass whereby bread and wine become the Body and Blood of Christ under the appearance or "species" of bread and wine, let us reflect on the following, Luke 24:13-35. After the resurrection, Jesus in his glorified body joins two discouraged disciples on the way to Emmaus. Because of Jesus' glorified body, the disciples do not recognize Jesus until significantly "the breaking of the bread." Notice the similarity between Jesus' words at the Last Supper (Lk. 22:19) and his words in Luke 24:30-31: "[W]hile he was with them at table, he took bread, said a blessing [this implies a change], broke it, and gave it to them. With that their eyes were opened and they recognized him, but he vanished from their sight." Jesus vanished from their sight, but his presence was recognized in the "breaking of the bread." To the disciples, Jesus was "made known in the breaking of the bread" (Lk. 24:35).

Today, in every Catholic Church, Jesus is made known to us in the "breaking of the bread," in his body and blood, in his Real Presence under the "species" of bread and wine.

By the Word of God Jesus became "flesh and blood" in the Incarnation. Likewise, by the Word of God—Jesus--bread and wine become "flesh and blood."

It is ironic that those who say they accept the Bible literally do not do so in the discourses on the Eucharist!

But why do we still call the Body and Blood of Christ "bread" and "wine"? The answer is simple: After the consecration the appearances or accidents of bread and wine remain, but the reality, the substance, is the sacramental Body, Blood, Soul, and Divinity of the resurrected Christ. Also, the "bread" of Christ reminds us of his presence in other ways (i.e., in the Scriptures, the will of God, the minister, the person, the sacraments, etc.).

Let us finish our discourse on the Real Presence with the words of the founder of Protestantism, Martin Luther (1517 AD). Even the founder of Protestantism had to admit to the historical truths of the Catholic Church's belief:

> *[None of the [early Christian writers] use such an expression as, 'It is simply bread and wine,' or 'Christ's body and blood are not present.' Yet [the subject of the Eucharist] is so frequently discussed by [the early Christian writers], it is impossible that they should not at some time have let slip such an expression as 'It is simply bread,' or 'Not that the body of Christ is physically present,' or the like, since they are greatly concerned not to mislead the people; actually, they simply proceed to speak as if no one doubted that Christ's body and blood are present. Certainly among so many fathers and so many writings a negative argument should have turned up at least once, as happens in other articles [of the faith]; but actually they all stand uniformly and consistently on the affirmative side' (Luther's Works, St. Louis: Concordia Publishing, 1961, vol. 37, 54).*

Even Luther could not deny history!

The Mass

Catholics have a Mass because Jesus instituted the Mass, and the early Church always had a Mass. Let us look at an example from Luke's Gospel:

When the hour came, he took his place at table with the apostles. He said to them, "I have eagerly desired to eat this Passover with you before I suffer, for, I tell you, I shall not eat it [again] until there is fulfillment in the kingdom of God." Then he took a cup, gave thanks and said, "Take this and share it among yourselves; for I tell you [that] from this time on I shall not drink of the fruit of the vine until the kingdom of God comes." Then he took the bread, said the blessing, broke it, and gave it to them, saying, "This is my body, which will be given for you; do this in memory of me." And likewise the cup is the new covenant in my blood, which will be shed for you (Lk. 22:14-20).

When we look at history, the Mass is a well-established reality for Christians. At first Christians celebrated Mass in their homes and with time they moved into public worship spaces, but the fundamental structure always remained the same.

It is astonishing to see in the year 150 AD, just 50 years after the death of the last apostle John, the existence in the Church of a set Mass structure that had to have been in place from the time of the apostles.

Justin Martyr, known by the friends of the apostles, wrote to the emperor Antononinus Pius in 150 about the long-standing practice of Christian worship in order to calm the anger and fear of the emperor in regard to the practices of the Christians.

Let us look at his description of the Mass in his letter:

On the day we call the day of the sun, all who dwell in the city or country gather in the same place, for it is on this day that the Savior Jesus Christ rose from the dead [In the early Church, according to Pliny, the Roman Governor of Pontus, in his Letters to the Emperor Trajan (ca. 111-113 AD,) the Christian faithful would often sing a "hymn to Christ as God" as they began their celebration of the "Lord's Supper."]

The memoirs of the apostles and the writings of the prophets are read, as much as time permits.

When the reader has finished, he who presides over those gathered admonishes and challenges them to Imitate these beautiful things.

Then we all rise together and offer prayers* for ourselves...and for all others, wherever they may be, so that we may be found righteous by our life and actions, and faithful to the commandments, so as to obtain eternal salvation.

When the prayers are concluded we exchange the kiss.

The faithful, if they wish, may make a contribution and they themselves decide the amount. The collection is placed in the custody of the one who presides over the celebration to be used for the orphans, widows, and for any who are in need or distress.

Then someone brings bread and a cup of water and wine mixed together to him who presides over the brethren.

He takes them and offers praise and glory to the Father of the universe, through the name of the Son and of the Holy Spirit and for a considerable time he gives thanks (in Greek: eucharistia) that we have been judged worthy of these gifts.

When he has concluded the prayers and thanksgiving, all present give voice to an acclamation by saying: "Amen."

When he who presides has given thanks and the people have responded, those whom we call deacons give to those present the "eucharisted" bread, wine, and water and take them to those who are absent (Apol. 1, 65-67; PG 6, 428-429).

In explaining the mystery indicated by the word

"eucharisted," Justin states in his *First Apology* (65):

> *We call this food Eucharist...since Jesus Christ our Savior was made incarnate by the word of God and had both flesh and blood for our salvation, so too, as we have been taught, the food which has been made into the Eucharist by the Eucharistic prayer set down by Him, and by the change of which our blood and flesh is nourished, is both the flesh and the blood of that incarnated Jesus.*

Justin further goes on to say:

> *None is allowed to share in the Eucharist unless he believes the things which we teach are true...for we do not receive the Eucharist as ordinary bread and ordinary wine, but as Jesus Christ our Savior.*

What you would have experienced in the year 150 and earlier is exactly what you experience today in any Catholic Church!

Mass as True Sacrifice

> *For I received from the Lord what I also handed on to you, that the Lord Jesus, on the night he was handed over, took bread, and, after he had given thanks, broke it and said, "This is my body that is for you. Do this in remembrance of me." In the same way he took the cup, and after supper, said, "This cup is the new covenant in my blood. Do this, as often as you drink it, in remembrance of me." For as often as you eat this bread and drink this cup, **you proclaim the death of the Lord** until he comes (1 Cor. 11:23-26).*

The expressions "This is my body," "this is my blood" are

taken from the Jewish language and theology of Temple sacrifice. For Jesus, these expressions designate himself as the *true and ultimate sacrifice.*

In the Old Testament, the Hebrew Scriptures, sacrifices of lambs, bulls, goats, and other animals were offered in the temple for the forgiveness of sins. Today, this sacrifice takes place in the mystery of the Mass, the bloodless sacrifice of the Lamb of God, Jesus Christ, at the altar of every Church, the New Temple of God. (It is no coincidence that John's Gospel has Jesus die at the exact time that the Jewish Temple sacrifices are taking place. It is Jesus who is the true Lamb, the true sacrifice. Jesus is the true Lamb who takes away the sins of the people).

The bloodless sacrifice of the Mass has traditionally been seen to have been prefigured in Genesis 14:18; 22:13, foretold in Malachi 1:10f, and attested to in 1 Corinthians 10:16, 18-21; 11:23-26 and Hebrews 13:10.

When the Jews were preparing for the Passover into the Promised Land, they offered up a paschal lamb and afterwards consumed the lamb, the victim, for strength for the journey (Ex. 12:1-20). This prefigures the Eucharistic sacrifice where Jesus, the Lamb of God, is offered up for our sins and then eaten sacramentally for the spiritual nourishment necessary for the journey into the Promised Land of Heaven.

The Mass is a *re-presenting*, or making present of what took place once and for all at Calvary (Heb. 7:27; 9:12, 25-28; 10:10-14). Just as the Passover meal made present to those who participated in it the Exodus events, the Mass in a fuller way makes present what happened at Calvary. As Gregory of Nyssa (ca. 383) in his *Sermon on the Resurrection* (4) explains:

Jesus offered himself for us, Victim and Sacrifice, and Priest as well, and 'Lamb of God, who takes away the sin of the world.' When did he do this? When he made his own Body food and his own Blood drink for his disciples; for this much is clear enough to anyone, that a sheep cannot be eaten by a man unless its being eaten be preceded by its being slaughtered. This giving of his own Body to his disciples for eating clearly indicates that the sacrifice of the Lamb has now been completed.

At every Mass Calvary is made present to us. Mass is a participation in that one and only sacrifice of Jesus on the cross at Calvary (cf. Heb. 7:27).

Our sin will not be small if we eject from the episcopate those who blamelessly...offered its Sacrifices (Clement, 4, trans. Jurgens). *.[W]e ought to do in order all things which the Master commanded us to perform at appointed times. He commanded us to celebrate sacrifices and services....at fixed times and hours* (Ibid., 40, trans. Lake).

Clement of Rome (ca. 80)

The Council of Trent would affirm, in opposition to the Protestant Reformation, the belief of the early Church regarding the sacrificial nature of the Mass.

[Christ] our Lord and God, was once and for all to offer himself to God the Father by his death on the altar of the cross, to accomplish for them an everlasting redemption. But, because his priesthood was not to end with his death (cf. Heb. 7:24, 27) , at the Last Supper, "on the night when he was betrayed" (1 Cor. 11:23), in order to leave to his beloved Spouse the Church a visible sacrifice (as the nature of man demands)"by which the bloody sacrifice which he was once and for all to accomplish on the cross would be re-presented, its memory perpetuated until the end of the world and its salutary power applied for the forgiveness of the sin

which we daily commit"; declaring himself constituted "a priest for ever after the order of Melchizedek" (Ps. 110(109)4), He offered his body and blood under the species of bread and wine to God the Father, and, under the same signs...gave them to partake of to the disciples (whom he then established as priests of the New Covenant), and ordered them and their successors in the priesthood to offer, saying: "Do this as a memorial of Me," etc., (Lk. 22:19; 1 Cor. 11:24), as the Catholic Church has always understood and taught.

[After Christ] celebrated the old Pasch, which the multitude of the children of Israel offered...to celebrate the memory of the departure from Egypt (cf. Ex. 12:1f), Christ instituted a new Pasch, namely himself to be offered by the Church through her priests under visible signs in order to celebrate the memory of his passage from this world to the Father when by the shedding of his blood he redeemed us, "delivered us from the dominion of darkness and transferred us to His Kingdom" (cf. Col. 1:13).

This is the clean oblation which cannot be defiled by any unworthiness or malice on the part of those who offer it, and which the Lord foretold through Malachi would be offered in all places as a clean oblation to his name (cf. Mal. 1:11). The apostle Paul also refers clearly to it when, writing to the Corinthians, he says that those who have been defiled by partaking of the table of devils cannot be partakers of the table of the Lord. By "table" he understands "altar" in both cases (cf. 1 Cor. 10:21). Finally, this is the oblation which was prefigured by various types of sacrifices under the regime of nature and of the law (cf. Gen. 4:4; 8:20; 12:8; Ex. passim). For it includes all the good that was signified by those former sacrifices; it is their fulfillment and perfection.... (J. Neuner and J. Dupuis, eds. The Christian Faith: Doctrinal Documents of the Catholic

Church, New York: Alba House, 1990), ND 1546-1547).

It is no coincidence that the Eucharist as the Body and Blood of Christ as well as Jesus' sacrifice and death on the cross were considered foolishness to many and a stumbling block to others (cf. Jn. 6:60; 1 Cor. 1:23). To believe in the Eucharist and in the death and resurrection of Jesus can only occur through a gift from God (cf. Jn. 6:65).

- The Greek for "Do this in memory of me" (Luke 22:19), *Touto poieite tan eman anamnasin*, can also be translated as "Offer this as a memorial offering." The *Didache* often applies the Greek word *thusia*, or sacrifice when referring to the Eucharist.

Prayers and Meditations

Medicine of Immortality

Your blessed saint, Ignatius of Antioch, called the Eucharist the "medicine of immortality, the antidote to death, and the food that promises everlasting life."

This medicine softens the hardened, heals the injured and makes humanity blossom.

This antidote brings back to life dead and distorted consciences--and repairs, offers forgiveness, and corrects the damages of sin.

O source and summit of the Church, O medicine of immortality, O food of everlasting life, may I draw life from you.

O source and summit of what I am meant to be, grant me the antidote of immortality, the medicine of everlasting life and spiritual health.

Come to Me

Come to me all of you who are weary.

Come to me and be nourished at my table.

Come to me and be nourished with the medicine of immortality, the pledge that you shall live forever.

Come to me, and receive your maker, your creator, the one who gave you life, and gave it abundantly.

Come to me, all of you, and make your soul a tabernacle, an ark for my presence.

Come to me all of you to the source and summit of Christian life, the source and summit of the grace that energizes that which is spiritually dead and renews the soul with hope and merit.

Come to me all of you and receive the fountain of life that brings sanctification and redemption, that brings comfort to pilgrim Christians and saints, and everlasting life.

Come to me all of you.

With You Always

"Behold, I am with you until the end of time" (cf. Mt. 28:20).

While you are present in many forms, your most intense, unique and profound presence is in your Eucharistic appearance.

On that holy evening so many years ago, to this very day, our pilgrim journey as people of God, as people of faith, hope and love, found and finds its source of strength in your sacramental presence.

It continues to be food for the journey and nourishment to strengthen us on our way to paradise.

It continues to be the source and summit of boundless love and Christian life—Christ himself, our Passover, our living bread and life-giving food.

"Behold, I am with you until the end of time" (cf. Mt. 28:20).

Body of Christ

Eucharistic body of Christ, sanctify me, convert me, drench me.

Eucharistic body of Christ, feed me, enlighten me, and be present to me in your "Eucharistic face."

Most holy body, blood, soul, and divinity of Christ, source and summit of what I am called to be, transform, convert, deluge, and drench me so intensely that I may be able to see as you see, to hear as you hear, to feel as you feel, to experience life as you experience it.

Inundate me with your Eucharistic presence.

O sacrament most precious, O saving presence, O saving food for the journey, be with me, in me, and for me.

Help me to make you all in all.

Foot of the Cross

O precious blood of Jesus, shelter and aid me in my times of sorrow.

Infuse in me the gift of strength and courage.

When I feel afflicted, bitter, abandoned, lonely and scorned, buffet me with the consolation of being embraced by your blood.

When I am inflicted by darkness and misfortune, permeate me with the blood of redemption and hope.

While the earth may shake, the heavens darken, your blood is there to be my comfort and shield.

O precious blood of Jesus, embrace and cover me.

The Lord's Veil

Almighty Lord, may you mold me with and by your precious body and blood into a docile instrument of your will.

May I see beyond the sacramental veil to see the Lord of lords, the King of kings, the master of heaven and earth.

May your precious blood saturate my eyes, ears, and speech so that I may see as you see, hear as you hear, and speak as you want me to speak.

May your precious blood inundate my arms, feet, my very being so that I may be your hands, feet, arms, your very life.

Almighty Lord, may you mold me with and by your precious body and blood into a docile instrument of your will.

May I see beyond the sacramental veil to see the Lord of lords, the King of kings, the master of heaven and earth.

Sharing in Calvary

Precious blood of Jesus, help me to carry my cross with you and for you.

Help me to unite my sufferings with yours, my flowing tears to your flowing blood, my climb upon my own cross with your climb, my suffering and bloodied life with your suffering and bloodied body.

Just as you suffer for me, with me, and in me, may I suffer in you, for you, and with you.

May I bleed as you bleed and in this mystery obtain the gift of redemption and salvation.

In Me, with Me, and for Me

O Lord, may I always be conscious of your Eucharistic presence.

May I always recognize that you are living in me, always present to me, always working for my good by moving and governing my entire being within the gift of your Eucharistic presence.

In your Eucharistic presence, you are always there to embrace me, sustain me, and enlighten me.

O Lord, may I always be conscious of your Eucharistic presence, your "Eucharistic face."

Sanctify Me

Precious blood of Jesus, sanctify me, purify me, sustain me.

O precious blood of Jesus, gift me with goodness, infuse me with hope, and sustain me in confidence.

Help me to observe your commandments, beatitudes, gifts and virtues.

Help me to listen to my conscience, to fulfill and submit to your will.

Precious blood of Jesus, sanctify me, purify me, sustain me.

Refresh My Soul

O blood of Christ, refresh my soul.

Washed and sent, help me to be a holy servant.

Stained by your blood, the blood of the new and everlasting covenant, help me to be a servant of servants within a community of servants.

May your precious stream of redemption, the blood poured upon the wood of the cross, refresh and save my soul.

Sacrament of Mystery

O precious sacrament of the paschal mystery, be the center of my life.

Help me to see in the sacrament of the altar the mystery of your life, death, and resurrection, the mystery of your crucifixion and burial, your conquering of death, and your coming into glory.

Help me experience the mystery of the eternal now, the mystery where all of history is accessible to the grace of redemption.

The world which came forth from your creative hands is now returned back to you, because of you, redeemed.

O precious sacrament of the paschal mystery, be the center of my life.

Rest at My Feet

I come, Lord Jesus, to your body and blood.

Heal me, divine physician, in my spiritual and physical ailments.

Quench my hunger and thirst, fountain and bread of life.

Make me, king of heaven, a servant of servants.

O graciousness, O sweetest and kindest Jesus, how wonderful you are to me.

How can I return that which cannot be returned, that which I can never receive worthily or devoutly enough, that which I can never venerate sufficiently.

How can I ever return your infinite goodness?

Help me, O Lord, return your gifts by resting below the cross, below your precious feet.

Upper Room

Make present to me the upper room, the paschal Triduum, the evening of Holy Thursday, the Last Supper, the feast of priests, the sacramental expectation of the agony in Gethsemane, the sweating of blood, the cross of Calvary, and the redemption.

Make present to me the cup of salvation and the bread of life that was lifted up for me.

Make present to me the hour of my redemption.

Help me to accept my "holy hour" as Jesus accepted his.

Help me to say, "Not my will, but thy will be done."

Help me to reach the deepest levels of loneliness and abandonment and find you, O Lord, at the very core of my being where my redemption was won.

Make present to me, O Lord, the upper room.

Communion Desire

Eucharistic Lord, you are all that I could ever desire and hope for.

You are my salvation and redemption, my hope and my strength, my honor and glory.

Help me to receive you with reverence and devotion, with humility and longing, with holy resolutions and spiritual joy.

Eucharistic Lord, you are all that I could ever desire.

Do not send me away hungry.

Nourish, nurture, and provide for me--as you make me one with you.

Eucharistic Lord, you are all that I could ever desire and hope for.

Gift of Gifts

The night of betrayal also became the night of the institution of the Eucharist, the inestimable gift, the *gift par excellence*.

This night brought the gift of Jesus himself, the gift of his sacred humanity, his saving work, his sacrifice, his passion, his death and resurrection.

The night of betrayal became a participation in the night that transcends all nights, the night of divine eternity.

In this eternal now, this divine eternity, the work of redemption continues inexhaustibly.

O love which knows no measure, which is mercy itself, mystery itself, life itself, bless me with the fruits that were instituted on that night so long ago.

May my nights never be nights of betrayal but nights of life.

May I never follow the ways of the betrayer but always follow the way of the savior.

May I never deny the gift of gifts, the gift *par excellence*, but may I always embrace the mystery of faith, the mystery of all mysteries, the mystery of life itself found in the medicine of immortality, the pledge that I shall live forever.

Bring me, O Lord, to the sacred banquet of communion and to the definite redemptive sacrificial place of my salvation made present ever anew.

Heavenly Hunger

You, O Lord, who prepared your body and blood for my food and drink, save me, receive me, and bring me to everlasting life.

Grant me an increase in devotion and a daily hunger and thirst for your body and blood.

Seek to Pierce

O Lord, help me to pierce with a lively, fervent, and hearty faith the reality which is you, the incarnate Word perpetually made present in the Mass.

Help me to see in your Eucharistic presence, your manifestation in the manger, your manifestation on the Mount of Olives, your manifestation on the cross and in your resurrection and ascension.

May I see you, the resurrected Christ, in your Eucharistic presence.

Grant me the graces through your sacramental presence to live the mystery I meditate upon, the mystery I seek to pierce.

Liquefy My Being

Precious blood of Jesus, liquefy my being with your love.

Cure me of my vices, spiritual ailments, unrestrained passions and temptations.

Precious blood of Jesus, pour forth your confirming faith, strengthening hope, and inflaming and engulfing love.

Precious blood of Jesus, sustain my frail body and soul, repair my human infirmities; grant me consolation and blessings.

Precious blood of Jesus, liquefy my being with your love.

Trials and Tribulations

Precious blood of Jesus, sustain and protect me in my times of trouble, in my times of trials and tribulations.

In my misery, lift me up.

In need, meet me.

In pain, heal me.

When wounded, bandage me.

In my feelings of abandonment and anxiety grant me comfort and peace.

Precious blood of Jesus, protect me and sustain me in your love.

Come to the Altar

I come to your altar, O Lord, with willing abandonment, simplicity of heart, obedience, servitude, contrition, penance, and perpetual praise.

I come to your altar and place upon it my sins and weaknesses, my desires and anxieties.

I come to your altar seeking reconciliation, the burning and consuming of my sins in the sacrificial fire of your love.

Wipe clean the slate of my conscience, and protect me from evil now and at the hour of my death.

May I come to your altar and learn to turn the other cheek. May I respond with love when people hurt me, offend me, abandon me, or inflict any injury upon me.

May I come to your altar to seek forgiveness for those whom I have burdened, grieved, troubled, or prevented from doing good.

Drive out from me suspicions, anger, dissensions and whatever wounds charity.

I come to your altar, O Lord, with willing abandonment, simplicity of heart, obedience, servitude, contrition, penance, and perpetual praise.

Source of Blessing

Mediator between God and humanity, source of every blessing, head and founder of the mystical body, cornerstone and fountainhead of genuine Christian devotion, high priest and shepherd of supernatural grace, primal source and final destiny of all things, unspotted victim, purifier and former of consciences, immaculate lamb, clean oblation, divine redeemer and sanctifier, free me from the shackles of all that hinders holiness.

Make me a partaker in your supernatural life, a participant in the life of thanksgiving, praise, supplication, and reparation-- make me a partaker in the life that leads me home to the Father.

May I come to the altar of my salvation professing faith, obedience to the divine law, and a participation in the sacrifice of my redemption.

Foster in me piety, kindle in me the flame of love, and augment in me a deep devotion.

May I come to the altar of salvation with a submissive mind fueled with holy zeal, fortified with energy, and intensified with holy works.

Bring me, O Eucharistic Lord, into a life of heroic virtue, a life of mystic union, a life disposed to receive you.

Bring me, O Lord of life, into a life of holiness.

Precious Blood

Precious blood of Jesus, drench and purify my heart, mind and body with the blood that sprinkled the Garden of Olives, that dotted the praetorian and streets of Jerusalem, that was shed at the crucifixion and spewed out on a lance.

Precious blood of Gethsemane, transfuse my will for your will.

Precious blood from the pillar of scourging, inundate me with your courage and strength in times of suffering.

Precious blood from the crown of thorns, overwhelm my soul with the ability to cope with humiliations, mockery, and persecutions.

Precious blood from the sacred heart, engulf my heart with a pure love of God, neighbor, self and creation.

Precious blood of Jesus, drench and purify my mind, heart and body with the blood that sprinkled the Garden of Olives, that dotted the praetorian and streets of Jerusalem, that was shed at the crucifixion and spewed out on a lance.

Transubstantiation

O divine gift, O source of every other gift, may I always worship you in your Eucharistic presence.

O mystery which surpasses all understanding, bless me with the gift of faith.

Transform my natural senses and give me mystical senses.

Transform my natural nature and make me supernatural.

Grant me, O Lord, the grace to see your body, blood, soul, and divinity in your "Eucharistic face."

O divine gift, O source of every other gift, may I always worship you in your Eucharistic presence.

Communion

In my communion with you, grant me an intimate sense of the spiritual reality I am receiving.

Aid me in grasping the reality of receiving the very one who offered himself for me on the cross, the very one who poured out his blood for the forgiveness of my sins, the very one who filled me with fire and the Spirit.

As I receive the mystery of mysteries, may I be nourished by your presence and your Spirit.

Nourish me with the food that purifies my soul, burns away my faults and blesses me with a sharing in the life of the Holy Spirit.

Nourish me, transform me, and form me into a communion that incorporates me so beautifully into you.

In my communion with you, grant me an intimate sense of the spiritual reality I am receiving.

Heavenly Liturgy

Nourish me, transform me, and form me into a communion of life that transcends this world and carries me into the heavenly liturgy.

Bring me into the presence of the angels, saints and your blessed Mother.

May we all cry out, "Holy, holy, holy Lord...Hosanna in the highest."

May I join the heavenly liturgy where heaven appears on earth and the earthly Church grasps the heavenly Jerusalem.

Grant me a foretaste of heavenly joy, of future glory, of fullness of life.

Assure me of the pledge of bodily resurrection and glorification at the end of this age.

Assure me, in communion, of life in the new heaven and the new earth.

May heaven and earth adore you now and forever.

Blood of Wounds

O precious blood of Jesus which flowed from your sacred wounds, anoint me, bless me, and heal my ailments.

Break through to my heart and pour out your gift of love and faith upon me.

Deliver me from evil and protect me from straying into harm's way.

O precious blood of Jesus, may the divine spring of divine mercy overwhelm and save me.

May it be the source of my strength and holiness.

O precious blood of Jesus flowing from your wounds, drench me, engulf me, immerse me, convert me, form me, and console me.

Flood the Soul

O precious blood of Jesus, flow into my soul, my heart, my very being.

Cleanse me of my sins.

Make me a source of reparation.

Guard my senses and sprinkle me with your presence.

O precious blood of Jesus, flow into my soul, my heart, my very being.

There for Me

O precious blood of Jesus, be there for me.

Be there for me in my own Gethsemanes, scourgings, crosses, and crucifixions.

O precious blood of Jesus, resurrect me and assume me into your sacred heart.

O precious blood of Jesus, be there for me.

Gaze

As you gaze upon me, may I gaze upon you.

As you hear me, may I hear you.

As you hunger and thirst for me, may I hunger and thirst for you.

As you move toward me, may I move toward you.

As you cherish and guide me in your providential hands, may I cherish you and guide you into my hands and into my heart at communion.

--May your words become my words,
    --your worship my worship
    --your sacrifice, my sacrifice.

As you gaze upon me, may I gaze upon you.

Eucharistic Fruit

Because of your passion and death I can experience holiness, consolation, strength and salvation.

Help me to recognize this reality.

Profoundly impress it upon my mind;

Make it present to my spirit;

Bless me with the fruits of the Mass, of communion, of adoration.

May I never lose sight of the importance of this paschal mystery, this passion, this mystery of life, death and resurrection.

Behind the Veil

Bless me with spiritual senses.

Help me to see beyond the veil,
--beyond the host,
--beyond your "Eucharistic face."

Help me to see you, O Lord, as fully human, fully divine, God and man.

And as I seek to see you beyond the veil, help me to see myself behind my own veil.

Help me see the core of who I am and who I am called to be.

May I see you behind the veil.

O Precious Drop

O precious drop of blood

--that redeemed and saved the world,
--that converted sinners and inflamed hearts,
--that brought faith and trust into the world,

--have mercy on me and on the whole world.

Transfigured

In this blessed Eucharistic communion of life and love, transform and transfigure me.

Help me to shine forth as an instrument of your love and renewal.

Renew in me a commitment to the building up of your kingdom, to the building up of a world dedicated to your honor and glory.

Help me to be a Eucharistic light to the world, a transfigured being seeking to transform a world hungering and thirsting for you.

In being nourished, transformed and transfigured by your presence may I work for peace, justice, and solidarity.

May I be there for the weakest of the weak and the poorest of the poor.

May I be another Christ in a world crying for Christs!

In this blessed Eucharistic communion of life and love, transform and transfigure me.

Incarnate Presence

In your incarnated presence you taught us how to pray and how to express our homage and dependence on the Father.

You taught us to pray through you, in the Spirit, and to the Father.

Teach me, O Lord, your humility, your perseverance.

Teach me to pray through my own agony in the garden, scourging at the pillar, crowning of thorns, carrying of the cross and crucifixion.

Teach me to prostrate myself and pray on my knees, with sighs of hunger and thirst for your body and blood.

In your incarnate Eucharistic presence, in your sacramental flesh, make me pure, devout, beloved.

Teach me, O Lord, teach me!

Teach Me

Teach me, O Lord, teach me.

Teach me, O Lord, to pray perfectly, to fulfill your will, and to do that which is for your honor and glory.

Teach me, O Lord, to see your reign, know your intentions, and clothe myself with your disposition.

Teach me, O Lord, teach me.

Precious Blood

Precious blood of Jesus, immerse me and the world in your salvific will.

Cover us all in your precious blood.

May we be drenched and embraced.

Help us to overcome obstacles, disordered affections, and dangerous occasions of sin.

O precious blood of Jesus, drench our thoughts, wills, and imaginations in your love.

Cover us and shield us from harm and empower us with zeal and devotion.

Help us spread your reign, your peace, and your Church throughout the world.

Precious blood of Jesus, immerse me and the world in your salvific will.

Daily Bread

"Give us this day our daily bread."

As you nourish my body, nourish my soul with the bread and wine of eternal life.

May this daily meal satisfy my hunger and quench my thirst.

May it nourish my thoughts so that they may be your thoughts, my affections so that they may be your affections, my works so that they may be your works.

O bread and wine of eternal life, O body and blood of Jesus, empower me to think as I ought, to discourse as I ought and to live as I ought.

Nourish my body and soul, my spiritual and temporal being—give me, I implore, this daily bread!

Self-Giving

O precious blood of Jesus, price of my redemption, pledge of salvation and eternal life, blood of the new and everlasting covenant, grant me your forgiveness and mercy.

O precious blood of Jesus, poured out for my salvation, bless me with the understanding of your supreme act of love and self-giving.

Bless me, sanctify me, consecrate me.

Will of the Father

O precious blood of Jesus, pour into my soul the heroic virtues, the beatitudes, the very will of the Father.

O precious blood of Jesus, be the source of my works and the source and summit of my Christian life.

O precious blood of Jesus, help me to be watchful in faith, firm in hope, fervent in love and rich in mercy.

O precious blood of Jesus, may I be that which I was meant to be—in your image and likeness.

Sacrament of Heaven

Grant me, O flesh of Christ, the gift of communion, perseverance, mortification, and a desire for heaven.

Bless my prayers and resolutions with the gift of assurance and hope.

Disengage me, O heavenly flesh of Christ, from the disorderly and worldly frivolities of this world.

O grant me, O flesh of Christ, a taste of heaven as I await my eternal destiny with you in paradise.

O Holy Sacrament

O holy sacrament, sacrifice of the cross, sacrifice of the new law, the new covenant, feed me.

O wondrous presence, abiding memorial of your passion, most wonderful of banquets, source and summit of reconciliation and salvation, be the food of eternal life for me.

O holy sacrament, proclamation of your life and death, of your ascension and self-giving love, may the immensity of your love for me be repaid by my own living sacrifice, my own perpetual memorial, my own self-giving love.

O wondrous presence, O holy sacrament, feed me in holy communion, in holy Mass, with the gift of becoming one with you and my neighbor, with the gift of grace and future glory.

Close to You

O Lord, in your "Eucharistic face," may I seek to spend time with you, to look upon you, and to adore you.

I seek to share my worries and anxieties, my sadnesses and joys, my every moments.

I seek to be close to your heart as the "beloved disciple."

I seek to experience that infinite love that flows from your heart--so ever present in your "Eucharistic face."

May your heart surge upon me the priceless treasure of the wellspring of your grace.

May my ear remain close to your breast as I acknowledge your love and presence.

May my very being remain so close to you that I may become a partaker in your divine nature, that I may become a person of faith, hope, and love, so that I may persevere in sanctifying grace and love, so that my heart and whole being may be united to you.

As I look upon your "Eucharistic face" may you illuminate my blind spots and give rise within my soul to a hunger for a deeper conversion within my life.

May I look upon your "Eucharistic face" with a pure conscience, a conscience filled with love and humility--and not with shame and obstinate sin.

In your "Eucharistic face" help me recognize the entire gift of salvation—one, holy, catholic, and apostolic.

O God, help me to see in Jesus' "Eucharistic face," his sacrifice, his resurrection, his ascension, his gift of the Spirit.

O precious Lord of life, grant me the grace that flows from the Eucharist as sacrifice, presence, and banquet--the gift of adoring, obeying, and loving you.

May I forever hear the words of the prophet Elijah: "Arise and eat or else the journey will be too difficult for you."

Mary of the Eucharist

Mary, Mother of God, Mother of the Church, Mother of the Eucharist, teach me the mysteries of your Son.

Help me Mary to experience the Eucharist as you experienced it.

Help me Mary to have your disposition of sheer abandonment to the mystery of faith, God made man, God made Eucharist.

Help me Mary to recognize that the same Son who changed water into wine is the same one who changes bread and wine into his body, blood, soul, and divinity.

As you, Mary, conceived the Son of God in your virginal womb, may we conceive sacramentally the Son of God in our souls through the Eucharist.

May I receive the same Jesus Christ, Son of God and Son of Mary, fully human, fully divine, under the signs of bread and wine.

May I receive in this sacrament the whole mystery of salvation.

Heart of Jesus

Heart of Jesus, pump your blood into me.

As I stand at the foot of the cross, may I ponder my eternal destiny.

"Look upon my wounds, my pierced hands, feet, and sacred heart," the Savior says.

"Look upon my humiliation."

"See my suffering."

"Experience my death."

"As you look upon me, dear child, what do you see?"

I see, O Lord, the price of my salvation.

Sacred heart of Jesus, pump your blood into me. May I love you as much as you love me.

Sacred Heart

Sacred heart of Jesus, teach me love.

Holy wounds of Jesus, heal my wounds.

Holy face of Jesus, help me to see as you see, hear as you hear, sense as you sense, speak as you speak, cry as you cry.

O five wounds of Jesus, heal and transform my physical and spiritual senses.

Sacred heart of Jesus, teach me love.

Blood of the Lamb

Blood of the Lamb, let not the angel of death harm me.

Be my safety, security, and freedom.

Heal and deliver me, for in your wounds I am healed, protected and saved.

My Fiat

May my "Amen" be like your "Fiat."

In your Magnificat, Mary, teach me the true meaning of praise and thanksgiving.

In imitation of you, Mary, help me accept Jesus in my heart even before I receive him sacramentally in my body.

Like you, Mary, may my life be completely a Magnificat!

May the same Word made flesh which dwelt in the tabernacle of your womb be the same Word made flesh present sacramentally in the tabernacle of my heart.

May the Christ who radiated through your eyes and voice to Elizabeth radiate through my eyes and voice.

As you looked upon the baby Jesus in the manger, grant me the gift of looking at Jesus in the sacrament of the altar.

As you, Mary, stood at the foot of the cross, may I find a place sacramentally at the foot of Calvary along with you.

As you received over and over again the Eucharistic meal of the very one you conceived as the spouse of the Holy Spirit, may I receive over and over again the sacramental presence of the mystery of all mysteries.

As I look intently on the host of salvation, may I hear inwardly the words of Jesus on the cross, "Behold your mother; behold your son."

Pour upon me from your side, Jesus, the grace to learn at the "school of Mary" and to allow her to accompany me and lead me into the life that she knew so well.

Grant me, O Mary of the Eucharist, your disposition toward your Son.

Sealed in Blood

Precious blood of Jesus flow through my being.

Flow into me physically, mentally, spiritually.

Cleanse my conscious and subconscious being.

Wash me in your blood--in my memory, my imagination and my will.

Cover my dreams, my sighs, my hearing and my thoughts.

A Walk

In your Eucharistic mystery you walk beside me and give me strength for the journey.

You give me hope, where there seems to be no hope, faith where there seems to be no faith, and love where there seems to be no love.

In your Eucharistic mystery you allow my heart to see what my eyes cannot--to know you so that I may adore you with unbounded faith, hope and love.

Prayer for Priests

Lord, protect and support your priests who are united in a singular and exceptional way to the Eucharist.

Lord, protect and keep faithful those who have been entrusted with this mystery of faith.

At the moment of the institution of the Eucharist your priests were born.

They were born to derive their strength and their very existence from the gift of the Eucharist.

At the moment of the institution of the Eucharist your priests found their very reason for being.

Dear Lord, may your priests manifest, in the celebration of the Mass, the depth of this mystery, the depth of this self-giving, the depth of this source and summit of their lives.

Soul of Church

Help me, O Lord, to make the Eucharist the center of my life, the soul of my Christian life.

Help me, O Lord, to enter into a sacramental communion with you, to enter into that communion that is the pledge of eternal life, that is the source and summit of what I am called to be.

Help me to be a good custodian of this sacramental encounter, this sacramental intimacy with you, O Christ.

Help me to experience this sacramental banquet which brings into existence the Church, the people of God.

Help me to receive you, to be nourished by you, to enter a life of grace and communion with you and your body, the Church.

Help me, O Lord, to make the Eucharist the center of my life, the soul of my Christian life.

Eucharistic Charity

O Eucharist, source of charity made present at every Mass, form me into your image and the image of your saints.

Open in my soul, "in spirit and truth," a real and unfathomable love that seeks to grasp your saving sacrifice.

May I see in your sacrifice love and may I respond to it in love.

May I not only know love, but may I begin to love as you love.

May I walk along the path of love that you have set before me, the path of progress, of development, of deep and strong growth.

May I see in your Eucharistic presence my most authentic and deepest Christian vocation of perfecting the image and likeness I was meant to be like, the image and likeness of you, O Lord.

Help me, O Lord, to be a sign of unity and a bond of charity in a world so hostile, cold and distant.

O sacrament of love, help me to fulfill the commandment of love of God and neighbor.

O Eucharist, source of charity made present at every Mass, form me into your image and the image of your saints.

Eucharistic Heart of Jesus

O Eucharistic heart of Jesus, may your heart speak to my heart.

At the Last Supper John reclined upon your heart.

At the foot of the cross your heart was pierced for John's sins and mine.

From the side of your heart, blood and water flowed out, signifying the gifts of baptism and Eucharist.

Grant me, O Lord, a love like that of John's.

Make me a person that chases after and seeks to be near your heart.

Make me love the image and likeness of you and your heart in the image and likeness of my neighbors.

O Eucharistic heart of Jesus, convert my hardened heart into a sacred heart.

O Eucharistic heart of Jesus, may your heart speak to my heart.

School of Love

I come to you, O Eucharistic Lord, to learn at the school of active love for neighbor.

Make me recognize the beauty of the Eucharistic mystery within my neighbor.

Educate me within the silence of my heart to love in a deeper manner.

Renovate me and teach me within the core of my being to authentically see the dignity of each person, especially those who suffer from injustices.

O Eucharistic mystery, teach me the truth about my inner self and the selves of others.

I come, O Lord, to learn at the feet of your "school of love."

Cleansing Bath

O precious blood of Jesus be a cleansing bath for my conscience.

Rinse my mind of any obstacles to introspection, self-reflection, and self-examination.

O precious blood of Jesus may I absorb you so that I may have the spirit and mind of the Church, the power of the Holy Spirit working within your Church.

O precious blood of Jesus, may your Words in Scripture, Tradition, and through your cloud of holy witnesses bless me with a concise vision of reality that corresponds to your will.

A Walk into Mystery

I have died many deaths on this earthly walk.

I have given all that I could until I could give no more.

I have cried out, "My God, my God, why have you forsaken me?"

Why has life dealt me such a blow?

I have no more to give.

O Eucharistic Lord, O blood divine, O food of immortality, O refuge of the sorrowful, shed your blood upon me as I walk into the unknown, into your mystery.

I surrender and trust.

Eucharist and Life

O Eucharistic Lord, animate me.

Act in me, with me, and for me.

Make me wholly, fully human.

May I recognize that in Eucharistic communion I live out the fullness of my call.

In you, veneration, love, charity, intimacy, spring forth to make me your disciple.

Fill my spiritual being, ensure its sacramental and physical life, ensure its salvation and its place within the journey of providence.

In Eucharistic communion, make me wholly, fully human.

Sancta Sanctis

In you, O Christ, the "holy things" are given to the holy.

In your action, O Lord, you, the holy one of God, anointed with the Spirit, consecrated by the Father, dying and rising for our sins, enter the sanctuary, the holy of holies, to act as the offerer and the offered, the consecrator and the consecrated.

In you, O Christ, the "holy things" are given to the holy.

Chalice of Salvation

We adore you, O Christ, O precious one, for you have shown us mercy.

You have spared, delivered, liberated, justified, redeemed, blessed, reconciled, pardoned, healed, made whole, and saved me in your blood.

I was once separated from you, now, through this chalice of salvation, this chalice of reconciliation, you wash me and help me to enter into a relationship with you.

You cover me with your precious blood of love.

Washed by your precious blood, O unblemished Lamb, continue to sanctify and sustain me.

Above All, Sacrifice

May I appreciate the sacrifice of redemption at every Mass, the sacrifice of the new covenant, the one and only sacrifice of Calvary where the then and now become one, where the sacrificial act of creation is brought back in the act of offering to the Father.

May I realize that in this Eucharistic sacrifice is found the mystery of love within the mystery of suffering.

Always and Everywhere

O Lord, may I always and everywhere be present to you as you are present to me in the tabernacles of the world.

May I always be blessed with the grace of always and everywhere being faithful to you as you are to me.

May I always be prepared to experience persecution for my love of your presence in the Eucharist as you so freely and lovingly suffered persecution for me.

May I always be present, always and everywhere, at the presence of your death as you will be at mine.

May I live always and everywhere in the presence of your Eucharistic presence, now and at the hour of my death.

My Love

O Jesus, may I love you in your sacramental presence above all worldly possessions and gifts.

Help me to see beyond the veil of your "Eucharistic face."

May I love you with devotion, attention, delicacy, confidence and respect.

Prepare my soul for love.

Help me through the gifts of prayer, penance, and mortification in order to correct and prepare myself to do your will in thought, word, and deed.

O precious Lord, you have always been there for me, loving me, sustaining me, raising me, bearing with me, encouraging me, and pardoning me.

May I love you as my creator, my savior, my holiness, and my happiness.

May I always be among your faithful sheep.

O Lord, may I love you in your sacramental presence.

Poured Out For You

On that night before you died, you gave me your body to nourish my hunger and your blood to quench my thirst.

As you feed and quench my needs, help me to shed and pour out my life for your people who hunger and thirst for you—as I hungered and thirsted for you.

Consecrated Offering

By virtue of the consecration, you come to us, O Lord, as the unbloody propitiatory offering to the Father on behalf of the world for its salvation.

In a supreme act of surrender and immolation, you, O Lord, have reconciled us to your Father.

In this consecrated offering you allow us to participate in your risen nature.

Thank you for allowing me to enter more perfectly through you, with you, in you, and in the unity of the Holy Spirit, into the life of the God who is all in all.

Kneeling before You

Before you, O Lord, I kneel.

I kneel before the crown of thorns, your pierced hands, feet, and side, your bloodied and bruised body.

Pour upon me the blood of life.

Strengthen my character, dominate my faculties, intermingle with my deeds and actions.

May I remain kneeling before you, bathed in your blood, as you tenderly mold and form my being and grant me the grace of salvation.

Quiet Rest

Precious Eucharistic Lord, grant me the grace to sit in your quiet presence before asking for or doing anything.

Grant me the grace to consult and confide in you always and everywhere.

Expose my inner being to the light of your pure love.

Purify my intentions and actions.

Help me know that I never labor alone and never in vain, that all I do in you and for you is meritorious and holy.

Precious Eucharistic Lord, grant me the grace to sit in your quiet presence before asking for or doing anything.

Mystery of Faith

O mystery of faith, O blessed Eucharist, given by you on that holy night so long ago, sanctify me.

You gave yourself to your spouse, your Church, as a pledge of your love.

O mystery of faith, O blessed Eucharist, O most precious treasure, O sacrament worthy of utmost devotion and veneration, O indissoluble bond between faith and devotion, help me to offer along with your new covenant priests this sacrifice for my salvation and spiritual nourishment.

O mystery of faith, O font of life, cleanse me, strengthen me, and live in me so that I may love you and my neighbor as I should.

O sacrament of love, O beginning of eternal life, O sign of unity, O bond of charity, O gift of grace, O pledge of future glory, reign in me.

O mystery of faith, O blessed Eucharist, given by you on that holy night so long ago, sanctify me.

Mystery

O precious blood of Jesus, permeate me with charity, a deeper conversion, the love of poverty, and the gift of wisdom and purity of heart, mind and body.

O precious blood of Jesus, infuse me with a desire to live out my baptismal vows, my life of consecration to you and your mother Mary.

Infuse me with your healing, sanctity and transformation needed to become your child.

O precious blood of Jesus, instill me with sorrow for my sins, perfect obedience to your will, a spirit of mortification and self-mastery, an ability to carry my daily crosses, and a healthy contempt for the world.

O precious blood of Jesus, impart in me a lively faith, hope, and love, a longing for heaven and a thirst for truth.

O precious blood of Jesus, fill me with a horror for sin, a love of the cross, and a pious transition from death to eternal life.

All for My Salvation

Feed my soul, O Lord, O God, O Creator, O Savior.

Only in you will my soul find rest.

Only you, O God, can feed my soul, can suffice it, satiate it, and fill it with what it truly and authentically needs.

You make a poor soul rich—all for my salvation.

You make a wanting heart warm, an insecure will firm, and uncertain mind lucid—all for my salvation.

You are a river for my thirst, a treasury in my poverty, a remedy for my ills, medication for preserving my being, and a cure for mediocrity and tepidity—all for my salvation.

May I hunger for you as you strengthen, beautify, rouse, and satiate my being—all for my salvation.

Feed my soul, O Lord, O God, O Creator, O Savior.

Only in you will my soul find rest.

O Lord of Hosts

O Lord of hosts, in you I live and move and have my being.

Because you live and move in me, you see and love in me what you see and love in yourself.

As your blood flows in my veins, your flesh is mingled with mine.

As I am united to you in your humanity, may I be united to you in your divinity.

Change me, O heart of life, O immortal and life-giving food; fill, penetrate, curb, influence, inspire every aspect of my being.

O Lord of hosts, in you I live and move and have my being.

Bathe and Cleanse Me

Precious blood of Jesus, bathe me and cleanse my soul.

Purify me of all imperfections.

Make my heart burn for you.

Precious blood of Jesus, help me to lose myself in the embrace of your love.

O balm of love, drown my sins in the sweet mercy of your tenderness and mercy.

Precious blood of Jesus, convert me, endow me with zeal, help me overcome my lukewarmness and grant me with bodily and spiritual health.

Precious blood of Jesus, bathe me and cleanse my soul.

Blood of Grace

Blood of grace, inform my faith, revive my hope, and fuel my love.

Precious blood of Jesus, imbue me with happiness in the depths of my being.

Protect me, shield me, cover me in your blood.

Dispose my soul with an ever renewed faith and hunger for truth, with an ever renewed fear of sin and judgment, and a fear of losing your life-giving presence.

Enrich my spirit, steady me in combat, purify my intentions, and kindle in me love.

Blood of grace, inform my faith, revive my hope, and fuel my love.

Here and Now

At every Mass, the mystery of the Eucharist, of the sacrifice of the Mass, of the mystery of Calvary, is recalled, re-enacted, re-presented.

What was so long ago is made present here and now!

Because your salvific act is present here and now, my sins can be forgiven here and now!

Moses made sacred his people through the blood of calves.

You, O Lord, make us sacred by your own blood in the institution of the Eucharist.

Taken, blessed, and broken I become yours.

Given for me, done for you, shed for me, done in memory of you.

At every Mass, the mystery of the Eucharist, of the sacrifice of the Mass, of the mystery of Calvary, is recalled, re-enacted, re-presented.

What was so long ago is made present here and now!

Sacred Heart

Below your bleeding sacred heart I kneel.

I cry for the wounds I have inflicted upon you by my sins.

Forglve me.

Help me to repent.

Help me to give my self, my whole self, without reservation or doubt to you and your cleansing bath.

My Lord and Savior, may the blood flowing from your sacred heart heal me, change me, strengthen me in body, soul, and spirit.

Cover me, O sacred blood, with your precious, saving and protecting armor of love.

Help me to love, praise, and thank you.

Help me to follow you every day of my life.

Below your bleeding sacred heart I prostrate myself.

I cry for the wounds I have inflicted upon you by my sins.

Forgive me.

Help me to repent.

Bathe me in your blood of mercy.

Five Wounds

Precious blood of Jesus that flowed from your sacred heart, cover me and drench me now and forever.

Precious blood of Jesus that flowed from your sacred hands uphold me in my journey of continual conversion and spiritual growth.

Precious blood of Jesus that flowed from your sacred feet keep me steadfast in my walk of faith, in my vocation of doing all for the honor and glory of the Father, and for building up Your kingdom.

Precious blood of Jesus that flowed from your pierced side, your sacred heart, help me to love and live as I ought.

Ransom for Many

O spiritual sacrifice, un-bloody act of worship, bring harmony and peace to your Church and your world.

Help the sick, comfort the afflicted, and assist all those in need.

Take pity on me and those who have gone before me marked with the sign of faith.

Have mercy on me, a sinner, and have mercy on those who have lost the sense of the divine and of sin.

Ransom my loved ones and all those who seemingly have no one to awaken them from their slumber of confusion and blindness.

O spiritual sacrifice, un-bloody act of worship, bring us light!

Laver of My Soul

Precious blood of Jesus, laver of souls, create me anew.

Precious blood of Jesus, worthy of all veneration, inflame me with faith.

Precious blood of Jesus, drained from your veins, empower me with hope.

Precious blood of Jesus, saving balm, well up in my soul so that I may be a fountain of your infinite love.

Precious blood of Jesus, laver of souls, saving balm, create me anew.

Precious blood of Jesus, transfuse your blood into my being.

Presence *par excellence*

O Lord, you are present to us in your Church.

When we pray, you pray with us, in us, and for us.

You pray as our priest, as our head, and as our God.

You, O Lord, are present in the authentic works of mercy, for what we do to ourselves and to others we do to you.

O Lord, you are present to us in your incarnate Word, your Gospel, your Church's preaching.

O Lord, Shepherd of shepherds, you are present to us in your bishops and priests as they rule and govern in your name and authority.

O Lord, you are present to us in your sacraments of initiation, healing and service, and most perfectly in the holy Eucharist, the source and summit of your Church's life and my Christian life.

In your Eucharistic face, your Eucharistic presence, you are there really, truly, substantially, wholly, entirely as God and man.

In your docility, in your teaching and praying Church, help me to comprehend these great and precious miracles of your love and presence.

In Eternity

What I now see in your "Eucharistic face" I will one day see in eternity most perfectly.

My life, my treasure, my love, my divine savior, under your Eucharistic veil enlighten my mind, stir up my heart, and inspire me with a firm hope, fervent faith, and burning love.

What humanity could never have conceived or uttered about you, O Lord my God, love has made manifest in your "Eucharistic face."

Food of Souls

Blessed Eucharist, food of souls, inestimable gift, all-powerful remedy against the world's tribulations, source of singular grace, assist me to meditate on your divine love, riches, and inexhaustible blessings.

Blessed sacrament, remain in my presence, day and night; be my consoler, savior, comfort, and relief.

In sickness and health, grant me merit.

In poverty of spirit, grant me humility.

In my battles against the world, the flesh and the devil, empower me to fight, resist, and win the victory.

O my God, O adorable heart, O sacred flame of love be my sweetness and tenderness.

Blessed Eucharist, food of souls, inestimable gift, all-powerful remedy against the world's tribulations, source of singular grace, assist me to meditate on your divine love, riches, and inexhaustible blessings.

Prepared for You

While the crown of thorns, the nails and the cross were being prepared, you, O Lord, were preparing a chalice and bread from heaven.

On the eve of the crucifixion, you were preparing your sacrament of love.

Amidst the turmoil and hatred of Jerusalem's populace, you were preparing an altar of immolation for us.

As people, rich and poor, strong and weak, prepared to eat the Passover meal, you gave us the food of immortality, the cup of salvation, the chalice of mercy, the fountain of grace, the ultimate Passover, the gift of eternal life.

Blessed Memorial

Bread of angels, heavenly food, memorial of your wonders, your power, wisdom and mercy, help me to consecrate my heart, mind, and will to praise and reverence the memorial of your wonders.

O Jesus of Bethlehem, Nazareth, Galilee, and Calvary be my food to nourish, feed, and satiate my soul, sweeten my sorrows, and receive me into eternity.

Inestimable grace, immense, incomprehensible divinity, wonder of wonders, grant me life everlasting.

Redeemer's Life-giving Flesh

O Lord, may I rejoice in your life-giving body and blood.

May I see in this mystery the body born of the Virgin, the body that hung on the cross for the salvation of all.

O Lord, may I rejoice in your life-giving body and blood, in your life-giving flesh.

Embalm me

Embalm me, O Lord, with your blood.

Precious blood of Jesus, inundate me with the love of you and my neighbor.

Satiate my being with a humble, gentle, mortified, charitable and modest spirit.

Precious Lord of grace, coat your blood upon my dangerous inclinations and impulses, diminish the fire of concupiscence, and take me along the river into holiness.

Precious blood, engulf me and embrace me in your providential love.

Embalm me, O Lord, with your blood.

Beneath the Veil

O Christ beneath the veil, invisible head of the Church, redeemer of the world, and center of all hearts by whom all things are and by whom all things exist, exert in me a desire to embrace a love for the common good, the community good, the good of the parish, the local church, the universal Church, and the entire world.

O Christ beneath the veil, may I be a cause of unity, a cause of ecclesial spirit where I may embrace the Church's cause as my own.

O Christ beneath the veil, contained, offered, and received, bless me with an ever-increasing love of this sign of unity, this bond of charity, this symbol of harmony, this price of salvation, this medicine of immortality, this source and summit of devotion, piety, veneration, and life for my soul.

O Christ beneath the veil, may I one day—in paradise-- come to see beneath the veil.

Foretaste of Heaven

Medicine of immortality, pledge of eternal life, securer of heaven, enter into my being, kindle it with glory, and create it impassible, agile, subtle, resplendent, and endowed with grandeur.

Adorn my soul with grace.

Free me from any inclination toward evil.

Help me to examine my conscience and inform it properly.

Precious blood flowing within me, expiate my sins as I shed tears.

Transfuse the poison of sin, with the medicine of immortality, your precious body and blood.

Convert me, transform me, transfuse me!

Endow me with a purity of life and an obedience of faith.

Bestow upon me, I beg thee, a taste of heaven here and now.

O Sacred Host

By the mystery of your Eucharistic presence, may I come to share in your divinity as you humbled yourself to share in our humanity.

O divine gift that comes from the very sacred heart of the redeemer, gift me with every kind of efficacious blessing.

O salutary fruit of redemption, elevate my human mind, bestow upon me the knowledge of the highest truths.

O sacred host, mode of union with humanity, summation and container of the supernatural order, strengthen my faith and fervor.

O measureless love for all, O immortal body of Christ, O seed of immortality, sustain me in adversity, strengthen me in the spiritual combat, and preserve me for life everlasting.

O means of support, bless me with perseverance.

O efficient cause of salvation, bestow upon me docility.

O sovereign cause of salvation, confer upon me your wisdom, your laws, your ordinances, your example.

O divine master, gift me with the inexhaustible abundance of your benefits of redemption.

O good shepherd, shepherd me into your kingdom, your paradise.

O most acceptable sacrifice, O symbol of concord, O sign of unity, bless me with a supernatural life.

O source of life, O very soul of the Church, assure me of the fullness of abundant life.

O word of life, help me to listen attentively to your Word and will.

O book of life, shaper of the course of human events, grant me confidence in your providential plan for me.

O bread of life, nourish me and sustain me on my journey, make me a sharer and partaker in your divine nature.

O most admirable sacrament, graft me unto your divine nature.

O crown of life, crown me with victory over death, with the attainment of the life of blessedness with God.

O food for the soul, unlike the food that becomes part of me, may I recognize that in your Eucharistic presence I am changed into you.

O source of the Church, source of all her strength, her glory, her every supernatural endowment and adornment, grant me every good.

O venerable sacrament, O point of rest, awaken and fire up my love toward you and my neighbors.

By the mystery of your Eucharistic presence, may I come to share in your divinity to the extent that you humbled yourself to share in our humanity.

Proper Shrine

Gift me with a pure intention as I approach your table, O Lord.

May I be a proper shrine for your presence.

May I come in humility and purity to the table of everlasting life.

May I come with a fervent desire to be united to you, so that I may become another you, another Christ in a world crying for Christs!

May the ends of my thoughts, desires, actions and undertakings find their conclusion in you.

May I approach your table with a proper attitude of gratitude.

May I live in my heart, mind, and will for the honor and glory of you and the building up of your kingdom here on earth--and at the end of my earthly pilgrimage join you, my savior, in eternity.

May I, dear Lord, be a proper shrine for you in a world crying for Christs!

Supreme Gift

O Lord Jesus Christ, your love is beyond explanation.

You not only became our brother, our savior, our God but you became our very source and summit of life.

You not only became like us in all things but sin in your Incarnation, but you also gave us the antidote for the poison of sin.

You not only saved our bodies and souls in your passion, but you also made yourself the sacrament of eternal life and spiritual nourishment.

O precious gift, O divine and supreme gift, your love for us is so great that you have given us the supreme gift of love, *your very self*, the holy Eucharist.

Gift of Love

Jesus had no wealth, no property, no home, no place to lay his head.

He left us with his cross, three nails, a crown of thorns, and his very self in the Eucharist.

He did not leave us with perishable goods, but imperishable wealth—eternal life won on Calvary.

He left us with his very self!   His very body and blood!

Maximum Miraculorum

O measureless love,

O infinite power,

O omnipotent force,

O wonder of wonders,

O *maximum miraculorum*,

--bless me with the gift of meditating and appreciating this greatest of gifts of love—the Eucharist.

O Holy Mass

O holy Mass relieve the souls in purgatory; bring blessing upon the world; give glory to God, and empower persons to be martyrs.

O holy Mass bring sorrow and contrition for sin and conversion of hearts.

O holy Mass, infinite in value, bring life to the dead, communion of peoples, and hearts, minds, and wills dedicated to your will and the great commission.

O holy Mass, source of grace, of healing, of perseverance and sanctity, bring refreshment, light, happiness, and peace to those marked by the sign of faith.

Not Known

O Lord Jesus Christ, I pray for all who do not know your sacramental presence in the Eucharist.

I pray for all those who do not know of your presence or have a wrong notion of it.

May my love for you make up for the lack of love by others.

Help me to think, speak, adore and receive you with the same anticipation that I received you at my first communion.

In the way I pray before you, adore you, and visit you, may the world know that you are present in the Eucharist—body, blood, soul, and divinity.

In my time close to you, in my reception of you, in my heart-to-heart talks with you, may my life reflect your Eucharistic face to the world.

May I express the Eucharist's sweetness and delights amidst a forgetful and cold world, a world that so often ignores your goodness.

Help me to return love with love.

In a world filled with superficial and lifeless faith, help me to enter into the heart of your Eucharistic presence.

O Lord Jesus Christ, I pray for all who do not know your sacramental presence in the Eucharist, who do not know you as the center of their hearts and the goal of their existence.

Publican, Thief, Centurion

Eucharistic Lord, may I have the heart of the publican, the good thief, the centurion.

Grant and bless me with the heart of the publican who cried in a sincere act of contrition, "Be merciful to me, a sinner."

Grant and bless me with the heart of the "good thief" who softened his heart, opened his eyes to his soul, and accepted his cross as an expiation for his sins and a victory over death.

Grant and bless me with the heart of the centurion, a soul filled with humility, gratitude, wonder and resolution, a soldier who cried, "I am not worthy to receive you, but only say the Word...."

Eucharistic Lord, may I have the heart of the publican, the good thief, the centurion.

Crying

Lord, help me to cry tears of sorrow when people do not see your sacrifice, your Calvary, your victimhood.

Lord, help me to cry tears when people do not see the reparation, sanctification, justification, and the merit you gained for us.

Lord, help me to cry tears when people fail to see your passion.

Lord, help me to cry when you are denied, abandoned and deserted, when fury and treachery are directed toward you.

O Lord, help me to cry when I am faced with Judases.

O Lord, help me to cry when your beautiful Eucharistic face is ignored and left alone.

Lord, help me to cry with tears of sorrow.

Eternal Blessedness

I am graced, O Lord, with eternal blessedness when I commune with you, the giver of immortality, grace itself, the Christ himself—body, blood, soul, and divinity.

As I partake of your sacramental body and blood--as it is eaten, poured out, and distributed for all--I am redeemed and saved.

The chasm between creator and creature is bridged.

The rift between heaven and earth is reconciled.

The fissure between life and death is destroyed.

In your body, blood, soul and divinity
--sickness is replaced with healing
--blindness with sight
--pride with humility
--covetousness with generosity
--lust with chastity
--anger with mildness
--gluttony with temperance
--envy with friendship
--sloth with diligence
--and death with life.

In your body, blood, soul, and divinity
--sinners are converted

--the ignorant are made wise
--the doubtful are reassured
--the sorrowful are comforted
--the wronged are given patience and consolation
--the injured are given strength to forgive and heal
--the dead are brought to life.

In your body, blood, soul, and divinity
--the hungry and thirsty are satiated and quenched with blessed immortality
--the disenfranchised are clothed, visited, sheltered and embraced by divinity itself, body and soul.

As I partake of your sacramental body and blood--as it is eaten, poured out, and distributed for all--I am redeemed and saved. The chasm between creator and creature is bridged. The rift between heaven and earth is reconciled. The fissure between life and death is destroyed.

Church Alive

In your body and blood, O Lord, you bless your people with faith, hope, and love.

You bless them with prudence, temperance, justice and fortitude.

You gift them with wisdom, understanding, knowledge, right judgment, courage, reverence, and the fear of hell and failing to love.

You bring, O Lord, to fruition your charity, joy, peace, patience, gentleness, goodness, meekness, and self-control.

In your body and blood, in your Eucharistic presence, you make us one, holy, catholic, and apostolic.

You make us Church!

Appendix
Rite of Eucharistic Exposition and Benediction

Exposition: After the people have assembled, a song may be sung while the minister comes into the sanctuary. Wearing a humeral veil he brings the Blessed Sacrament from the place of reservation. It is placed in a monstrance, with candles on the altar, an altar cloth, and a purificator. The following song may be sung:

O salutaris Hostia
Quae coeli pandis ostium
Bella premut hostilia
Da robur fer auxilium.

Uni trinoque Domino
Sit sempiterna Gloria
Qui vitam sine termino,
Nobis donet in patria.
Amen.

During the song, or shortly after, the priest incenses the Blessed Sacrament.

Adoration: During the exposition there can be prayers, songs, and readings directed toward instilling a greater worship of Christ the Lord. A homily may follow. Religious silence is also highly recommended.

Benediction: *The priest or deacon goes to the altar, genuflects, and kneels. While kneeling, the minister incenses the Blessed Sacrament in the monstrance. The following song may be sung during this time:*

Tantum ergo Sacramentum
Veneremur Cernui;
Et Antiquum documentum
Novo cedat ritui;
Praestet fides supplementum
Sensuum defectui

Genitori Genitoque
Laus et iubilatio
Salus, honor, virtus quoque
Sit et benedictio:
Procendenti ab utroque
Compar sit laudatio.
Amen.

> **V.** **You have given them Bread from heaven. Alleluia.**

> **R.** **Having within it all sweetness. Alleluia.**

Minister rises, sings or says:

Let us pray. Lord, Jesus Christ, you gave us the Eucharist as the memorial of your suffering and death. May our worship of this sacrament of your

body and blood help us to experience the salvation won for us and the peace of the kingdom where you live with the Father and the Holy Spirit, one God, for ever and ever. Amen.

The humeral veil is placed on the priest or deacon. He goes to the altar, genuflects, and takes the monstrance and elevates it over the people, making the sign of the cross. Afterwards, the divine praises may be said:

Blessed be God.
Blessed be His Holy Name.
Blessed be Jesus Christ, true God and true man.
Blessed be the Name of Jesus.
Blessed be His most Sacred Heart.
Blessed be His most Precious Blood.
Blessed be Jesus in the Most Holy Sacrament of the Altar.
Blessed be the Holy Spirit, the Paraclete.
Blessed be the great Mother of God, Mary most holy.
Blessed be her holy and Immaculate Conception.
Blessed be her glorious Assumption.
Blessed be the name of Mary, Virgin and Mother.
Blessed be St. Joseph, her most chaste Spouse.
Blessed be God in His angels and in His saints.
Amen.

<u>Reposition:</u> *The Blessed Sacrament is replaced in the Tabernacle and the priest genuflects. Meanwhile, the* *people may sing or say an acclamation, and the minister then leaves.*

O Sacrament Most Holy
O Sacrament Divine,
All praise and thanksgiving
Be every moment Thine,
Be every moment Thine.

Holy God, we praise thy name,
Lord of all, we bow before thee,
All on earth thy scepter claim,
All in heaven above adore thee,
Infinite thy vast domain,
Everlasting is thy reign.

Infinite thy vast domain,
Everlasting is thy reign.

Made in the USA
Middletown, DE
25 October 2016